BOOK ANALYSIS

Written by Nathalie Roland
Translated by Jessica Foster

AF131399

Utopia

BY THOMAS MORE

THOMAS MORE

ENGLISH LAWYER, PRIVY COUNCILLOR, HUMANIST AND THEOLOGIAN

- **Born in London in 1478**
- **Died there in 1535**
- **Notable works:**
    - *Utopia* (1516), novel
    - *Epigrammata* (1520), collection of poems
    - *Supplication of Souls* (1529)

Born in London in 1478, Thomas More went on to study law. Elected as a Member of Parliament in 1504, he got married, had four children and acquired the position of undersheriff (local law enforcement) of London. He subsequently became part of Henry VIII's Privy Council and undertook several diplomatic missions to France and the Netherlands: these enabled him to meet humanists of the time such as Guillaume Budé (1467-1536) and Erasmus (c. 1479-1536). He also visited monks and became very familiar with the Bible. He was an enemy of English Reformers and renounced their heresy in many writings that were published between 1529 and 1532. He was a devout Catholic and therefore refused to approve Henry VIII's remarriage. He was convicted of high treason, beheaded and died.

UTOPIA

JOURNEY TO THE LAND OF NOWHERE

- **Genre:** novel
- **Reference edition:** More, T. (2012) *Utopia*. Trans. Baker-Smith, D. London: Penguin Classics.
- **First edition:** 1516
- **Themes:** society, politics, justice, equality, government, reason

Utopia appeared for the first time in 1516 and was soon highly successful. To go with *In Praise of Folly* that his friend Erasmus of Rotterdam had dedicated to him in 1509, he imagines a land governed by wisdom, a land which therefore exists "nowhere". He presents the text as the tale of the journey of an explorer in a strange land. Using this device, he begins a critique of English society, incomparably inferior to this ideal land where justice, equality and happiness reign. He thus created the utopic genre which would continue to inspire authors for centuries to come.

SUMMARY

Thomas More wrote a text in which he tells the story of a friend, Raphael Hythloday, for another friend, Peter Giles (Flemish humanist, 1486-1533). He asks Peter to verify the story's accuracy, as he wishes for there to be no untruths in the book.

FIRST BOOK

More first describes the circumstances in which he met Peter Giles and Raphael Hythloday in the Netherlands. The latter had been travelling with Amerigo Vespucci (Italian explorer, 1454-1512) and stayed in a distant country with his travelling companions after the explorer left. After establishing links with the natives, he visited their country, Utopia. He tells his two friends about his adventure. More is interested in the ways and customs of Utopia, believing that some of them are "patterns [that] might be taken for correcting the errors of these nations among whom we live" (p. 14). Giles tells Hythloday that, on account of his experience and his knowledge, he could become a councillor to the king, but the latter refuses this possibility. He tells a long anecdote that illustrates how badly his decisions have been received in England.

During a dinner with Cardinal Morton, one of the guests commends justice and the tough repression directed towards thieves. In disagreement with this, Hythloday explains that people who have become disabled in wars, impoverished by taxes, or peasants who have lost their land to rich people have no choice but to beg or steal. Furthermore, he states that it is unjust and against the law of God to kill someone for stealing. He notably draws upon the case of Persia, where a thief gives the stolen property back to its owner before being sent to do forced labour: in his opinion, this law is more "mild and gentle" (p. 34). While no one seems to agree with this sentiment, the Cardinal recognises that this could solve the problem of vagabonds.

The three friends continue their conversation on kings and their entourages. Based on the theories of Plato (Greek philosopher, 427-348/7 BC), More is convinced that a prince must be surrounded by philosophers. He believes that a prince must have practical knowledge of philosophy: it must be "more pliable, [know] its proper scene, [accommodate] itself to it" (p. 51). Hythloday mentions the situation in Utopia and details the benefits of the community of goods. They have a break to eat before Hythloday describes this strange land.

SECOND BOOK

Hythloday begins with a geographical description of the island, describing its size, its terrain, its port, its entrances, its headlands, etc. After this, he briefly explores its history before stating that "the manners, customs, and laws of [the 54 cities] are the same" (p. 63). He then describes the capital, Amaurot, near the river Anider, where all the houses look identical.

He then discusses the political organisation: there is a senate, with the people's representatives, and a prince, elected by secret ballot. He states that "no conclusion can be made in anything that relates to the public till it has been first debated three several days in their council" (p. 72).

The inhabitants all work in agriculture, whether they are city-dwellers or not, but each of them mostly focuses on the work they enjoy. They make their clothes themselves. Days are divided into 24 hours, of which six are for work. As no one is unemployed, it does not take long to create objects that are useful to everyone.

In order for the population to remain stable in every city, married girls go to live with their husbands' families. If the number of people living on the island becomes too large, colonies are created. The social order is well-established: wives obey their husbands, children obey their parents, the young obey the old.

The Utopians eat their meals together, preceded by a short moral lecture and accompanied by music. In the country-side, due to the distance between the houses, everyone eats at their own place. Permission is required to go and eat in another house.

The inhabitants do not use money and are contemptuous of gold and silver, which they use to make chamber pots.

All the children are educated by books and school, and speak the national language. Hythloday has noticed that their ancestors made almost the same discoveries as ours and that, in philosophy, they are trying to figure out the roots of human happiness.

As for religion, they reward virtues and punish vices. They believe in the immortality of the soul, which God has destined for happiness. This happiness can be found in "true or real pleasure" (p. 109). Therefore, this means living in harmony with nature, taking care of oneself and of others, etc.

During a discussion, Hythloday and his travelling companions introduce the Utopians to the Greek language, which is very similar to their own, and teach them to create a printing works and paper. They thus publish several works.

The Utopians have slaves, who are either citizens who have committed a shameful act, or foreigners condemned to death whom they have freed. They look after the sick considerately, but if someone has an incurable disease, they are offered euthanasia.

Punishments are decided by the senate on the basis of each wrongdoing. They prefer to reduce wrongdoers to slavery instead of killing them as this way they are useful to society. In Utopia, there are not a great number of laws and all the inhabitants know them all. They "are promulgated for this end, that every man may know his duty" (p. 134).

Utopians detest war and only fight in their defence. Before conflict, they always try to negotiate and if that does not work, they prefer to fight using cunning and trickery.

Most Utopians are monotheists: they believe in Mithras,

the "one Supreme Being that made and governs the world" (p. 155). But the legislator Utopus implemented freedom of beliefs in order for peace to reign. Priests are elected, live in their temples and only speak on things that are agreed upon in all religions. Hythloday and his companions introduce them to Christianity and convert a number of them.

To Hythloday, this commonwealth is "the best" and "the only commonwealth that truly deserves that name" as "all men zealously pursue the good of the public" (pp. 175-176). There are no poor people or beggars. Justice reigns and work is rewarded. At the end of the text, More seems to have been enticed by the way of life in Utopia: "there are many things in the commonwealth of Utopia that I rather wish, than hope, to see followed in our governments" (p. 183).

CHARACTER STUDY

PETER GILES

A mutual friend of Erasmus and Thomas More, Peter Giles first worked as an editor for the printer Dirk Martens (1450-1534) before becoming the registrar of the city of Antwerp in 1510. He prepared the first edition of *Utopia* that was published in Leuven by Thierry Martens (Flemish printer, 1453-1534) in 1516. As the work states, More and Giles met during a diplomatic mission in the Netherlands. More describes him by emphasising his friend's humanist qualities as well as his good and learned nature. More dedicates *Utopia* to him: this is a way for the author to ensure his work is protected by a friend, whom he asks to check the accuracy of his story. He is a secondary character in the dialogue and does not intervene a great deal.

RAPHAEL HYTHLODAY

Hythloday is a fictional character and was, More explains, introduced through the intervention of Peter Giles. He is described as an old Portuguese man with a long beard (a distinctive sign of philosophers) and a tanned complexion, whose appearance resembles that of an explorer. The etymology of his name in Greek means 'expert in folly'. He is the narrator and storyteller of life in Utopia. This is a device used by More, partly to make his story believable (Hythloday travelled with Amerigo Vespucci), and partly to distance himself from his creation (More invented nothing: all he did was dutifully repeat what Hythloday said). Fascinated by the Utopian institutions, he doubts the Europeans' ability to change theirs.

THOMAS MORE

Although he is the author of Utopia, More presents himself through his titles and qualities of being citizen and under-sheriff of the city of London. In the dedication, he describes himself: he seems to be a man who is extremely invested in his professional tasks and an intellectual who would like to spend more time studying, but also someone who considers family and friendship to be very important. He confides in Peter Giles his fears surrounding the publication of his work and the criticism it could receive. As the privileged spokesperson for Hythloday, he rarely interrupts the story, only asking questions from time to time. Firstly, he states the importance of practical philosophy for princes. Secondly, he defends the ideas that dominated at the time surrounding private property.

ANALYSIS

HISTORICAL CONTEXT

Political crisis: the Italian Wars (1494-1559)

Italy was made up of different independent, rival states, and therefore had been a very important location for foreign powers since the 15th century. The Italian Wars saw the clash of the Valois of France with the Habsburgs (who were in power in today's Spain, the Netherlands, Belgium, Germany and Austria) for the possession of the Kingdom of Naples and the Duchy of Milan. In 1511, England joined the League of Cambrai: this was a coalition that fought the claims of France in northern Italy. It was made up of Pope Julius II (1443-1513), King Ferdinand II of Aragon (1452-1516), the Republic of Venice and Swiss mercenaries. In 1514, Henry VIII (1491-1547) left the league and pledged peace with France. But a year later, on account of the ambitions of the new French king, Francis I (1494-1547), Henry VIII got closer to Spain. In 1516, Charles of Habsburg (the future emperor Charles V, 1500-1558) succeeded Ferdinand to the throne of Spain and the Netherlands. Charles soon became the enemy of France and notably allied with Henry VIII to be elected ruler of the Holy Roman Empire in 1519.

These numerous conflicts led to diplomatic missions to deal with various problems or to forge alliances. Thus More describes the diplomatic mission that he undertook for commercial reasons in Flanders or criticises the ambitions of the French in Milan.

Religious crisis: the Reformation

In the 16th century, different schools of thought called the Catholic faith and its members into question (denouncing the Pope's greed and the clergy's vices), and wanted to return to a religion that is closer to its original principles. This was the beginning of the Reformation, which affected all of Europe and led to many feuds and wars. In his work, More gives a possible solution: the legislator Utopus has established the principle of religious freedom to avoid conflicts.

Another upset: the discovery of the New World

From the first half of the 15th century, Portugal and Spain set about conquering oceans and new lands. Discovered in 1492 by Christopher Columbus (1450/1-1506), the New World was mapped out by Amerigo Vespucci, who is also mentioned by More. This is the start of colonial empires and a global economy: trading posts are constructed and maritime routes are created to transport goods and riches (food, gold, etc.). Europe discover that other people exist. Travellers tell stories of more or less real relationships and these are very popular among readers at the start of the 16th century. Utopia appears in this context of exoticism and discovery.

The particular case of Henry VIII's England

In the 15th century, civil wars between two English royal families (the War of the Roses) divided the country. At the end of the conflict (1485), many soldiers found themselves unemployed and wandered the countryside. Additionally, following some significant discoveries, the economy was no longer based on agriculture, but on trade and urban industries, notably the wool trade. Farmers are therefore removed from large spaces of public land, which are replaced with private sheep farms: this is known as the Inclosure Acts. In *Utopia*, More realistically describes the extreme situation of this impoverished population, forced into vagrancy.

GENRE: UTOPIA, AN IMAGINARY WORLD

Definition

A utopia (which in Ancient Greek means 'land of nowhere') is the imaginary creation of a society in which the author sets out new rules and ideal institutions with a view to transforming the world as he knows it. In his work, Thomas More criticises English and Western society in the 16th century and offers a model based on uniformity, equality and pooling resources.

Reading *Utopia*, however, we wonder: is the utopia real or fictitious? On the one hand, the author uses many elements that make this a work of fiction: the name of the island means 'nowhere'; the main river (Anider) is, according to its etymology, 'without water'; the name of Hythloday, the explorer and testifier to this land, means 'expert in folly', etc. On the other hand, Utopia might seem real. Indeed, the humanist recounts the story of the journey in detail and with expertise, frequently referring to real people. The reader also notices that miracles, fantasy and magic are not used.

Characteristics

In 1516, Thomas More is the first to use the term 'utopia' as a noun (which is now a proper noun). He therefore gives rise to the utopic genre and to some of its characteristics:

- A utopia is generally situated on an island (the inhabitants therefore live withdrawn into themselves without external influences);
- The Utopians despise gold and silver (gold chamber pots, p. 96);
- The economy relies solely on agriculture (pp. 64-65);
- The utopia functions with regularity which is particularly noticeable in the geometric layout of the town (pp. 67-70);
- Time in the utopia seems immobilised: the past seems long ago, and almost mythical and there is no more progress as the organisation is already perfect (p. 74);
- A legislator (Utopus in More's case) is responsible for the utopia: he has implemented social uniformity which leads to equality of all the citizens and the elimination of social classes (uniformity of clothes, p. 74);
- There is a form of state intervention that does not leave much room for individualism or personal choices: everything must be done in the name of the community (collectivism) with the aim of reaching collective happiness;
- No one in Utopia may remain unemployed;
- The Utopians give great importance to education, a major concern of humanists.

Origin and evolution of the utopic genre

Although More is the first to use the term 'utopia', the origins of the utopic genre date back to Antiquity, specifically to Plato. Between 384 and 377 BC, the Greek author wrote

The Republic, a work in which he imagines an ideal city. But Christianity also offers other examples of the utopic genre: several Bible passages, such as earthly paradise, take place in an ideal world. Moreover, faced with the problems posed by Medieval towns (problems with circulation and hygiene), Renaissance intellectuals reflected upon the characteristics of ideal cities.

Inspired by the Italian Leon Battista Alberti's (1404-1472) treatise on architecture, they tried to organise towns practically (from the point of view of transport and security) and aesthetically (symmetrically or in the shape of a square or star, etc.).

Following Thomas More, many authors would continue to use the utopic genre: *The City of the Sun* (1602) by Tommaso Campanella (Italian writer and philosopher, 1568-1639), *The Adventures of Telemachus, the Son of Ulysses* (1699) by François Fénelon (French clergyman and writer, 1651-1715), *Gulliver's Travels* (1726) by Johnathan Swift (Irish writer, 1667-1745), *Paul et Virginie* (1789) by Bernadin de Saint-Pierre (French writer, 1734-1814), *The Mysterious Island* (1874) by Jules Verne (French writer, 1828-1905), etc. In the 20th century, we also see the rise of anti-utopias such as *Brave New World* (1932) by Aldous Huxley (British writer, 1894-1963) or *1984* (1949) by George Orwell (British writer, 1903-1950).

THOMAS MORE, A HUMANIST

Thomas More's humanism can initially be described as committed humanism: in the same way as the first Italian humanists, he had different positions in the political and judiciary domains throughout his career. On the other hand, he is also connected to Christian humanism: he was involved in the religious controversies of his time, fighting the Reformation, even if in *Utopia* his message is more tolerant.

Good to know

Humanism was a trend in Italy in the 13th century before spreading throughout Europe until the 16th century. It was a movement of complete renewal in literature, arts and thought. Intellectuals revived the knowledge of Antiquity (a glorious past unlike the Middle Ages, considered to be dark and lacking interest) and made more space for people, reconciling these two ideas with Christianity.

Other elements of Utopia attest his attachment to humanist ideas. More makes several references to Antiquity:

- He alludes to real or fictitious characters from Greek and Roman Antiquity but also from Christianity and Oriental culture: Odysseus, Cicero, Moses or Mithras.
- He establishes the religious principles of the Utopians by using two contemporary philosophical trends from Greece in the 4th century BC as his basis: hedonism and stoicism. Both aim to obtain peace of the soul but differ on how to get there. In the opinion of Epicurus (Greek philosopher, 341-270 BC) and his followers, the wise man should lead a virtuous life, but one that is also made up of natural and necessary pleasures. In the opinion of the

Stoics, the wise man must master his passions, and accept the order of things and his place in society by fulfilling his duty. Additionally, Stoics believe in reincarnation and therefore do not eat meat.

- He is inspired by Plato's ideas, notably in his reflection on an ideal city, when he mentions the necessity of the presence of philosophers in the prince's inner circles or when he advocates equality for all in the eyes of the law.

More also gives a great deal of importance to education, in the same way as other humanists of his time, particularly for the prince. An example of this is the list of 'classics' he cites as needing to be known. He also has a deep respect for human life: "for nothing in the world can be of equal value with a man's life" (p. 29). Finally, much like other humanists, he criticises war, a "very brutal thing" (p. 140).

UTOPIA: A TREATISE ON POLITICAL PHILOSOPHY FOR GOVERNORS

In *Utopia*, Thomas More puts forward his ideas for a better form of governance, based on several principles, namely goods, uses, nature and reason.

- In politics, he advises the prince to have a philosophical education and to be surrounded by good advisors, but he also recommends a system of demographic representation of the population.
- As for society, he places family and happiness at the heart of his concerns.
- Regarding law and justice, he recommends having a small

number of laws, which are thus known by everyone, and the abolition of the death penalty.

- With regard to religion, although he promotes religious tolerance, he believes it is necessary to believe in something.
- As for war, he suggests it only in self-defence or defence of allies; and in these cases only as a last resort.
- Regarding foreign policy, he rejects the principle of treaties, favouring a system of alliances and mutual exchanges.
- In relation to money and sharing goods, he proposes a system in which private property and money no longer exist, thus allowing the pooling of goods and their equal distribution.

FURTHER REFLECTION

SOME QUESTIONS TO THINK ABOUT...

- Define a utopia. What does Thomas More do to create this other world and bring it to life?
- With the help of a table, compare the customs of the inhabitants of Utopia with those of England. Is the situation better in Utopia? Explain your answer.
- Which ideas and humanist ideas does More defend in his work? Explain.
- Specialists believe that *Utopia* belongs to political philosophy. In your opinion, why is this?
- What methods does More use to attempt to escape criticism that could be directed towards his work? Explain your answer.
- In your opinion, does living in Utopia mean living in democracy? Explain your answer.
- Are the values and behaviour of the Utopians in line with the religious context of the time?
- What literary and historical references does more draw upon to create *Utopia*?
- Compare More's *Utopia* with other works from the same genre. Do you see any recurring elements?
- Could this book be described as a travel story? Justify your answer.

We want to hear from you!
Leave a comment on your online library
and share your favourite books on social media!

FURTHER READING

REFERENCE EDITION

- More, T. (2012) *Utopia*. Trans. Baker-Smith, D. London: Penguin Classics.

REFERENCE STUDIES

- Desbazeille, M. M. (1998) *Utopia. Thomas More*. Paris: Ellipses.
- Marc'Hadour, G. (1992) *Thomas More. Un homme pour toutes les saisons*. Paris: Éditions ouvrières.
- Trousson, R. (1975) *Voyages aux Pays de Nulle part. Histoire littéraire de la pensée utopique*. Brussels: Éditions de l'ULB, pp. 50-62.
- Utopia. The Exhibition. [Exhibition] BnF (National Library of France). Available from: http://expositions. bnf.fr/utopie/anglais/enimages/aindex.htm

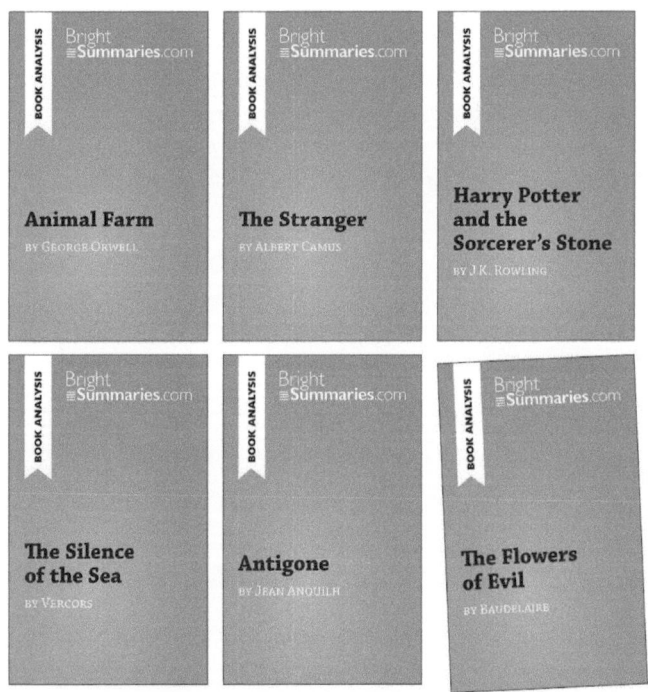